THE SCARIEST PLACES ON EARTH

ST. LOUIS
CEMETERY NO.1

BY MICHAEL FERUT

BELLWETHER MEDIA · MINNEAPOLIS, MN

Are you ready to take it to the extreme?
Torque books thrust you into the action-packed world
of sports, vehicles, mystery, and adventure. These
books may include dirt, smoke, fire, and chilling tales.
WARNING : read at your own risk.

Library of Congress Cataloging-in-Publication Data

Ferut, Michael.
  St. Louis Cemetery No. 1 / by Michael Ferut.
    pages cm. -- (Torque: The Scariest Places on Earth)
  Summary: "Engaging images accompany information about St. Louis Cemetery No. 1. The combination
of high-interest subject matter and light text is intended for students in grades 3 through 7"-- Provided by
publisher.
  Audience: Ages 7-12.
  Audience: Grades 3 to 7.
  Includes bibliographical references and index.
  ISBN 978-1-60014-997-9 (hardcover : alk. paper)
  1. St. Louis Cemetery #1 (New Orleans, La.)--Juvenile literature. 2. Haunted cemeteries--Louisiana--
New Orleans--Juvenile literature. 3. Ghosts--Louisiana--New Orleans--Juvenile literature. I. Title.
  BF1474.3.F47 2014
  133.1'2976335--dc23
                                    2014003687

This edition first published in 2015 by Bellwether Media, Inc.

Printed in the United States of America, North Mankato, MN.

TABLE OF CONTENTS

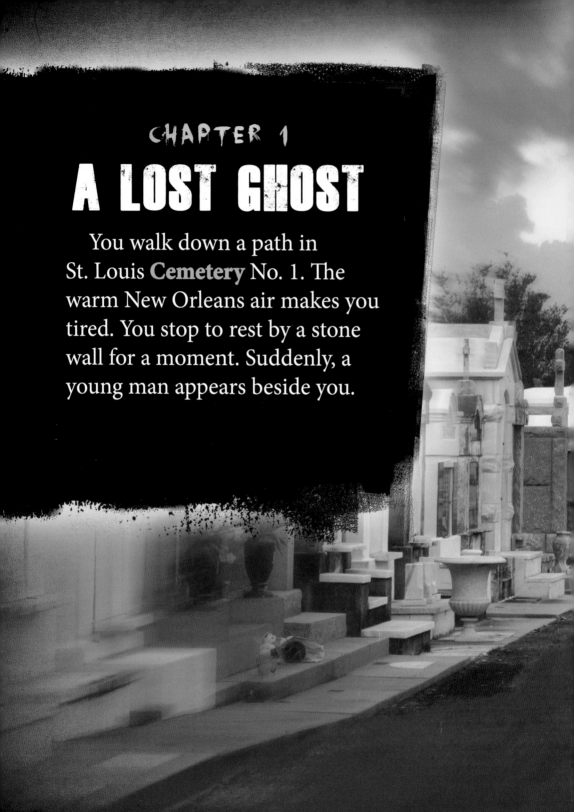

CHAPTER 1

A LOST GHOST

You walk down a path in St. Louis **Cemetery** No. 1. The warm New Orleans air makes you tired. You stop to rest by a stone wall for a moment. Suddenly, a young man appears beside you.

He says he is lost and cannot find his way home. You tell him you are just a visitor. As you walk away, he grabs your arm. His hand is ice cold.

You shiver as you turn to face him. But when you look, he is gone. Who was that man?

CHAPTER 2
CITY OF THE DEAD

St. Louis Cemetery No. 1 was opened in New Orleans, Louisiana in 1789. It is the oldest existing cemetery in the city. It was built after the Great New Orleans Fire of 1788.

When people first moved to New Orleans, they buried the dead underground. However, the ground was very wet and floods sometimes uncovered bodies. This made some people sick. The city started to use aboveground **tombs** to prevent this and save space.

Louisiana

New Orleans

ROOM FOR ONE MORE?

In this cemetery, a body stays inside a coffin for a year. Then the coffin is removed from the tomb to make room for another body. The bones are put in a bag and stay in the tomb.

There are about 700 graves in St. Louis Cemetery No. 1. Most hold many bodies. In total, around 100,000 people are buried there.

The tombs are packed together in one city block. Narrow alleys wind between them. People call it the City of the Dead because the cemetery looks like a small town.

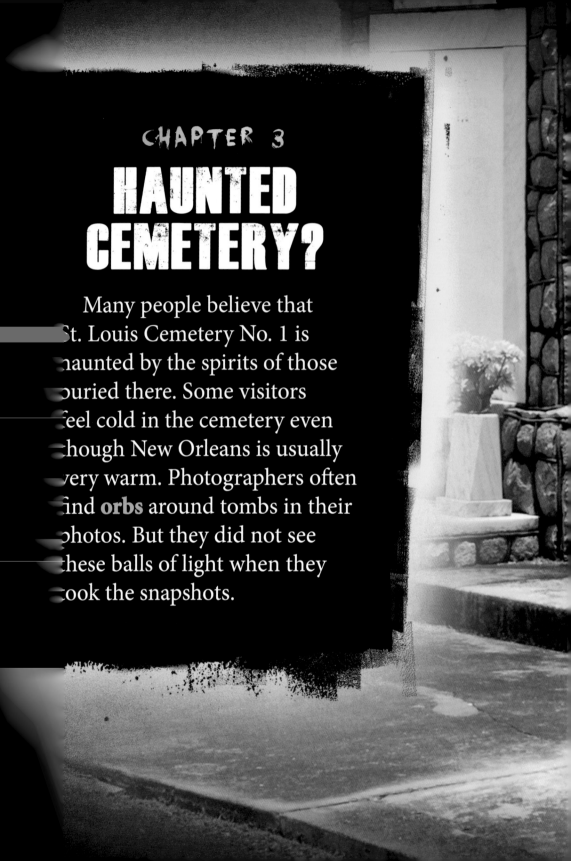

CHAPTER 3

HAUNTED CEMETERY?

Many people believe that St. Louis Cemetery No. 1 is haunted by the spirits of those buried there. Some visitors feel cold in the cemetery even though New Orleans is usually very warm. Photographers often find **orbs** around tombs in their photos. But they did not see these balls of light when they took the snapshots.

PET CEMETERY

Visitors also report seeing ghost dogs and cats. These animals are the pets of past caretakers. They are believed to be waiting for their owners to feed and care for them.

13

The ghost of Marie Laveau is said to haunt St. Louis Cemetery No. 1. She was a Creole woman who lived in the 1800s. People called her the Voodoo Queen. She was famous for her magic.

People often claim that Marie's ghost roams the cemetery and curses visitors. When they approach her, she vanishes. Sometimes she takes the form of a black cat with red eyes. Many think her daughter also haunts the cemetery.

XXX MARKS THE SPOT

Some people believe Marie still grants wishes. They do things like knock on her tomb and mark it with three Xs. Many people also leave gifts

Some visitors think one man's spirit haunts the cemetery because he was not buried in the right place. As the story goes, a sailor named Henry Vignes bought a tomb. But when he was away at sea, it was sold without his approval. He was buried instead in an unmarked grave. His ghost still searches for his rightful resting place.

FREAKY FARE

A cab driver once claimed he drove a woman in a white dress from the cemetery to a nearby house. But she disappeared before they arrived. The man at the house believed it was his dead bride.

18

Thousands of people come to St. Louis Cemetery No. 1 each year to walk its winding paths. Many of its tombs are in very bad condition. Some are **vandalized**. Many say this disturbs the spirits.

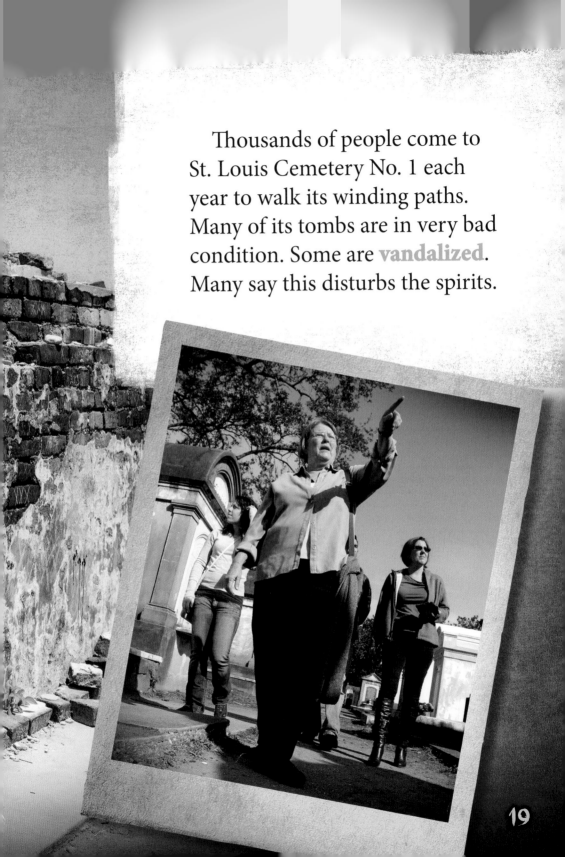

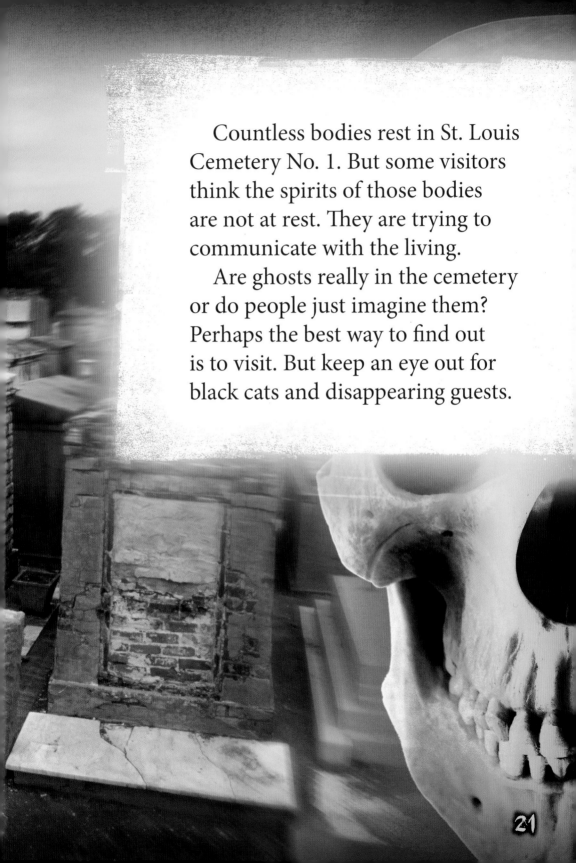

Countless bodies rest in St. Louis Cemetery No. 1. But some visitors think the spirits of those bodies are not at rest. They are trying to communicate with the living.

Are ghosts really in the cemetery or do people just imagine them? Perhaps the best way to find out is to visit. But keep an eye out for black cats and disappearing guests.

cemetery—a place where the dead are buried

city block—a rectangular area of land surrounded by streets

Creole—people with a mix of African, French, and Spanish heritage; Creoles are often from the southern United States or the Caribbean.

curses—wishes for bad things to happen to people

orbs—balls of light

tombs—chambers where dead bodies are placed for burial

vandalized—damaged on purpose

vanishes—disappears

voodoo—a religion from Africa; people who practice voodoo worship their ancestors and many gods.

TO LEARN MORE

AT THE LIBRARY

Polydoros, Lori. *Top 10 Haunted Places*. North Mankato, Minn.: Capstone Press, 2012.

Stone, Adam. *Ghosts*. Minneapolis, Minn.: Bellwether Media, 2011.

Williams, Dinah. *Spooky Cemeteries*. New York, N.Y.: Bearport Pub., 2008.

ON THE WEB

Learning more about the St. Louis Cemetery No. 1 is as easy as 1, 2, 3.

1. Go to www.factsurfer.com.

2. Enter "St. Louis Cemetery No. 1" into the search box.

3. Click the "Surf" button and you will see a list of related web sites.

With factsurfer.com, finding more information is just a click away.

INDEX

The images in this book are reproduced through the courtesy of: Scott A. Burns, front
cover (top), pp. 2-3 (background), 18-19; Andria Patino/ Alamy, front cover (bottom),
pp. 4-5; Croisy, front cover (skull); BB_Image, p. 6 (woman); Zack Frank, pp. 6-7
(background), 8-9 (background); Juan Martinez, pp. 8-9 (map); David Lowrey, pp.
10-11; Jon Eppard, pp. 12-13 (composite), 16-17 (composite); iofoto, p. 14 (left); Dirk
Ercken, p. 14 (right); Splash News/ Newscom, p. 15; Associated Press, p. 19; Marka/
SuperStock, pp. 20-21.